Modern World Religions

Sikhism

Jon Mayled

Heinemann Educational Publishers
Halley Court, Jordan Hill, Oxford, OX2 8EJ
a division of Reed Educational and Professional
Publishing Ltd

OXFORD MELBOURNE AUCKLAND
JOHANNESBURG BLANTYRE GABORONE
IBADAN PORTSMOUTH (NH) USA CHICAGO

Heinemann is a registered trademark of Reed
Educational and Professional Publishing Ltd

First published in 2002

06 05 04 03 02
10 9 8 7 6 5 4 3 2 1

British Library Cataloguing in Publication Data
A catalogue record for this book is available from the
British Library

ISBN 0 435 33626 6

Picture research by Jennifer Johnson
Typeset by Artistix, Thame, Oxon
Illustrated by Artistix
Printed and bound in Spain by Edelvives

Acknowledgements
The publishers would like to thank the following for
permission to use photographs:

The Environmental Picture Library/Graham Burns, p. 50;
TRIP/H. Luther, pp. 45, 56; TRIP/Resource Foto, p. 48;
TRIP/H. Rogers, pp. 2, 5, 6, 7, 8, 9, 10 (right), 12, 13, 19,
20 (both), 21, 23, 24, 25, 28, 29, 49, 52, 54, 55, 58, 59;
Harjinder Singh Sagoo, pp. 3, 10 (left), 14, 15, 18, 26, 27,
30, 31, 32, 33, 34, 35, 36, 37, 38, 40, 41, 42, 43, 44, 46, 47,
53, 57; TRIP/R. Westlake, p. 51.

The publishers have made every effort to contact
copyright holders. However, if any material has been
incorrectly acknowledged, the publishers would be
pleased to correct this at the earliest opportunity.

Websites
Links to appropriate websites are given throughout the
pack. Although these were up-to-date at the time of
writing, it is essential for teachers to preview these sites
before using them with pupils. This will ensure that the
web address (URL) is still accurate and the content is
suitable for your needs. We suggest that you bookmark
useful sites and consider enabling pupils to access them
through the school intranet. We are bringing this to your
attention as we are aware of legitimate sites being
appropriated illegally by people wanting to distribute
unsuitable and offensive material. We strongly advise
you to purchase suitable screening software so that
pupils are protected from unsuitable sites and their
material. If you do find that the links given no longer
work, or the content is unsuitable, please let us know.
Details of changes will be posted on our website.

Tel: 01865 888058   www.heinemann.co.uk

Contents

An introduction to Sikhism

In this section you will:

● learn about and understand what faith and trust mean

● consider how Sikhism seeks to strengthen faith in Waheguru (God)

● think about the aims of Sikhism.

Faith and trust

The people who follow **Sikhism** are called Sikhs. The word 'Sikh' means a disciple, someone who follows the teachings of a

Poster showing the ten Gurus and the Guru Granth Sahib JI

leader. In Sikhism, these are the teachings of the **Gurus**.

All Sikhs have faith and trust in God, called **Waheguru** – Wonderful Lord, the God who created all things.

Like all other religions, Sikhism is based on a system of **beliefs**. Beliefs are things that people think to be true, even if there is little evidence to support the beliefs.

Believing in something means that a person has **faith** and **trust** in what they believe. Faith is a firm and honest belief, that goes beyond all else. Trust is the certainty that what a person believes is right, a complete confidence in something, or a certainty that we will not be let down. For example, we may trust our friends.

Sikhs believe that their religion is a complete way of life. They believe that God created all things, and also that God has given guidance to help all people to live good lives. So, to be a true Sikh means to accept God and to carry out God's will.

Sikhism teaches that no one is better than anyone else. One of the main aims of Sikhism is that there should be a united human society living together in peace and equality and following the teachings of God. In particular, Sikhs believe in **sewa** – selfless service for others.

Sikhism gives freedom of thought to all believers. It aims to help people reach **mukti**, so that they can escape from being reborn again and again. To reach mukti they must show love and obedience to God.

Sikhism aims to free people from vanity and greed, from envy and tension, from fear and insecurity. Sikhism also aims to free people from the worship of false gods and low desires, and shows them the beautiful hope of goodness and excellence which leads to freedom. Sikhism fills the heart with love for God and for all God's creation.

Sikhs are certain of their faith because God has told people about Waheguru through the teachings of the Gurus.

The first of these Gurus was **Guru Nanak Dev Ji**. To show respect to the Gurus, Sikhs add the words Ji or Dev Ji, meaning 'Honoured Sir' to the names of the Gurus.

The word Guru has two syllables – the first, 'gu', means darkness and the second, 'ru', means light. A Guru is, therefore, someone who helps others pass from darkness to light.

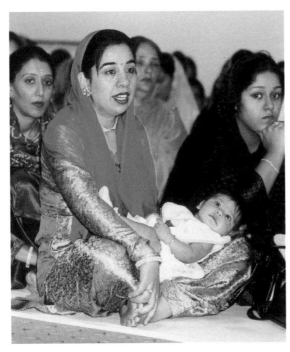

Sikh women in the gurdwara

Learning about religion

❶ a   In pairs, discuss the meaning of 'faith' and 'trust'.

   b   Write down your ideas and discuss them with the class.

❷   How do you think faith, trust and friendship help strengthen a Sikh's belief in God?

❸ a   Write down the main aims of Sikhism.

   b   Add other aims to your list as you work through this book.

Learning from religion

❶ a   Make a list of people who you trust.

   b   Why have you chosen these people?

❷   What effect does faith have on people's lives?

❸   How might the world be different if people did not trust each other?

Guru Nanak Dev Ji 1

In this section you will:
● begin to learn about the Sikh Gurus
● find out about the early life and teachings of Guru Nanak Dev Ji.

Sikhism is the youngest of the six major world religions: Buddhism, Christianity, Hinduism, Islam and Judaism. It was founded by **Guru Nanak Dev Ji** in the fifteenth century.

The Sikh faith came from the teachings of the ten **Gurus**. They are all respected by Sikhs, but not worshipped because they were human beings, not gods.

Sikhs believe that the Gurus were all very special people who did not need to be reborn, but were sent back to earth to become God's messengers.

The Gurus taught that there is only one God, that all people are equally important before God and that everyone can attain **mukti** (freedom) if they live their lives with love and are faithful and obedient to God.

Guru Nanak Dev Ji's childhood

Guru Nanak Dev Ji was born in 1469 CE at Talwandi in the Punjab. Talwandi was later renamed Nankana Sahib in his honour and is now in Pakistan.

When he was born the astrologers said he would grow up to be someone special who would lead others towards God.

Map of north-west India showing the modern-day Punjab

Nanak's father, Mehta Kalu, was a Hindu and so brought up his son to follow this religion. When he was still young, Nanak did not accept the many rituals and customs of Hinduism.

When he was five years old he was sent to school. His teacher, Gopal Das, wrote the letters of the alphabet on a slate and Nanak asked what each letter meant. The teacher said that the letters themselves did not mean anything and asked Nanak what he thought the letters meant. Nanak went through the alphabet and used each letter as the start of a verse of poetry in praise of

God. This hymn can be read today in the Sikh scriptures, the **Guru Granth Sahib Ji**. The teacher realized that Nanak was no ordinary child, but a messenger of God.

When a Hindu boy reaches the age of about eleven years old he is given a sacred thread to wear. Nanak refused to wear it, saying that a thread could break, and what he wanted was 'that sacred thread which after the death of a man accompanies his soul to the next world'.

He said: 'Make kindness the material, and spin the thread of contentment. Tie knots of truth and virtue. These qualities in a person are the real sacred thread.'

On one occasion, Nanak's father sent him to a nearby town and gave him some money which he was told to spend wisely. On the way he met some holy men. He asked them how they could live without food, homes or jobs. The men told him that they had no need of these things because God provided for them. Nanak thought about this and when he arrived at the town he spent his money on food for the men.

When Nanak returned home his father was angry because he had intended that his son should invest the money not give it away.

Guru Nanak Dev Ji – the first Guru

Learning about religion

❶ a In pairs, discuss the meaning of 'respect' and 'worship'.

   b Write down your ideas and discuss them with the class.

❷ a Describe one important event from Guru Nanak Dev Ji's early life.

   b What made people think that Nanak was a very special person?

❸ Explain why Nanak's teaching about the sacred thread was so important.

Learning from religion

❶ What do you think are the right ways to use money?

❷ Explain why it might be important to give money to others.

❸ Do you think the world would be different if more people followed Nanak's example? Why?

Guru Nanak Dev Ji 2

In this section you will:

- understand the importance of Guru Nanak Dev Ji's life and work
- consider Sikh teachings about equality
- express your own opinions on some of the aims of Sikhism.

One of the most important events in the life of **Guru Nanak Dev Ji** happened when he was 30 years old. Early every morning, Nanak went to the river to bathe and to pray. One day he did not return at his usual time. His friends went to the river and found his clothes on the bank, but there was no sign of Nanak. Three days later, he reappeared at the same place, but said nothing about what had happened to him.

This event had a great effect on his life. Guru Nanak Dev Ji left his home and family and travelled around the country teaching and preaching.

Guru Nanak Dev Ji taught that everyone should worship the same God and that every person was equal and should be treated equally. He said that there was 'no Hindu and no Muslim because everyone was equal in God's eyes'.

He said that people should always be prepared to work hard in order to serve God. He taught that human life is our chance to meet the creator, God, through having absolute love and devotion to **Waheguru**.

Guru Nanak Dev Ji also taught that arrogance, pride, lust, anger, greed and concerns about possessions all take us away from God.

Guru Nanak Dev Ji visited many holy Hindu places on his travels, including Varanasi in India

Guru Angad Dev Ji – the second Guru

He taught that rituals, idol worship, prejudice about people's **caste** (the belief that people are born into different groups), and any type of oppression, including the oppression of women, was wrong.

In 1520 CE Guru Nanak Dev Ji went to live in the village of Kartarpur in the Punjab and here he set up the first Sikh community.

A man called Bhai Lehna was making a pilgrimage to a Hindu shrine when he met Guru Nanak Dev Ji.

Lehna decided to visit Guru Nanak Dev Ji. He was wearing his best clothes. The people were gathering grass in the fields and there was one muddy bundle left. Lehna carried it to the village. Guru Nanak Dev Ji's wife was horrified to see the visitor carrying the bundle, but Guru Nanak Dev Ji told her that it was not a bundle of grass but 'a crown to honour the best of men'.

After this, Lehna served Guru Nanak Dev Ji in every way he could. Guru Nanak Dev Ji found Lehna to be the 'purest of the pure', and chose him above his own two sons.

He blessed Lehna, giving him the name Angad, which means 'part of me'. Bhai Lehna was now known as Guru Angad Dev Ji, the second Guru.

Learning about religion

❶ What do you think might have happened when Guru Nanak Dev Ji disappeared?

❷ What was so important about Lehna picking up the muddy bundle of grass?

❸ a Write down what Guru Nanak Dev Ji said about Lehna.

   b Explain why Guru Nanak Dev Ji chose Lehna to be his successor.

Learning from religion

❶ a What does Guru Nanak Dev Ji's statement 'There is no Hindu and no Muslim' mean?

   b How do you think this statement might be put into practise?

❷ Explain why it might be important today for people to avoid arrogance, pride, lust, anger, greed and concerns about possessions.

❸ What lessons could people learn from Guru Nanak Dev Ji's teachings?

The Gurus 1

In this section you will:

● learn about the lives and teachings of some of the other Sikh Gurus

● consider how their example might influence people's lives.

Below we look at the four **Gurus** who followed **Guru Nanak Dev Ji**.

Guru Angad Dev Ji (1539–52)

Guru Angad Dev Ji collected together all the hymns of Guru Nanak Dev Ji and wrote them down, along with some of his own, in the **Gurmukhi** script.

Guru Angad Dev Ji encouraged Sikhs to take part in sport regularly. He believed that a healthy body and a healthy mind were both important to God.

Guru Amar Das Ji (1552–74)

Bhai Amar Das was 60 years old when he met Guru Angad Dev Ji. He was a Hindu, but the teachings in the Guru's **shabads** (hymns) made him see that God could only be served through true devotion and love and so he changed his whole way of life. He served Guru Angad Dev Ji for thirteen years.

Every day he collected water from the River Beas for the Guru's bath.

Guru Amar Das Ji became Guru when he was 73 years old. He encouraged the use of the **langar**, or Guru's kitchen, to carry on Guru Nanak Dev Ji's idea of communal eating. He also asked his followers to come to his headquarters in **Goindwal** three times a year on the dates of important Hindu festivals.

Guru Ram Das Ji (1574–81)

Guru Ram Das Ji founded the sacred city of **Amritsar**. He was the son-in-law of Guru Amar Das Ji, and took over from him in 1574 CE at the age of 40. Guru Ram Das Ji invited people from 52 different trades to come to Amritsar and start new businesses in the 'Guru's Market'. He also composed the **Lavan**, which is a special hymn sung at Sikh weddings. He died at the age of 57.

Guru Arjan Dev Ji (1581–1606)

Guru Arjan Dev Ji was the fifth Guru, and the youngest son of Guru Ram Das Ji.

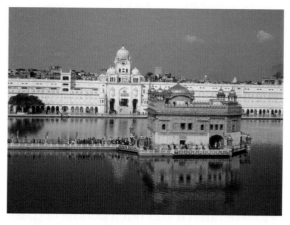

The Golden Temple at Amritsar

Guru Arjan Dev Ji

Guru Arjan Dev Ji built the **Harimandir Sahib** (the Golden Temple) at Amritsar.

Guru Arjan Dev Ji collected the hymns of the first four Gurus, together with some of his own, in a volume called the **Adi Granth**. Once the Adi Granth was completed and placed in the Harimandir Sahib, Guru Arjan Dev Ji slept on the floor of the temple to show his respect for the word of God.

Guru Arjan Dev Ji was the first Sikh martyr. The Mogul emperor was jealous of the Guru and tried to convert Guru Arjan Dev Ji to Islam under the threat of death.

Guru Arjan Dev Ji refused and was tortured and killed. The torture lasted for five days. The Guru was placed in a tank of boiling water. The next day, he had to sit on a plate of red-hot iron. On the third day, red-hot sand was poured over his body. Guru Arjan Dev Ji remained calm and peaceful to show that all people should happily accept the will of God. Before his death, Guru Arjan Dev Ji sent a message that his son Har Gobind was to become the sixth Guru. He said that, because peaceful means had failed with the emperor, it was now right to use the sword to protect the weak and innocent.

Learning about religion

❶ a Explain the main events in the life of Guru Arjan Dev Ji.

b Why were the events of his life so important?

❷ Describe how Guru Amar Das Ji served and respected Guru Angad Dev Ji.

❸ Why do you think that Guru Amar Das Ji encouraged his followers to visit him three times a year?

Learning from religion

❶ a Why might God want his followers to have a healthy body as well as a healthy mind?

b Do you think that people should put this idea into practise today? Why?

❷ Explain why it might be important to serve other people in the way that Guru Amar Das Ji served Guru Angad Dev Ji.

❸ Explain what lessons could be learnt from the example of Guru Arjan Dev Ji.

The Gurus 2

In this section you will:

● learn about the lives and teachings of some more of the Sikh Gurus

● consider how their example might influence people's lives.

Below we look at the four **Gurus** who followed Guru Arjan Dev Ji.

Guru Har Gobind Ji (1606–44)

Guru Har Gobind Ji was the only son of Guru Arjan Dev Ji. He was eleven years old when his father was executed and he became the sixth Guru.

Guru Har Gobind Ji is sometimes called the 'Warrior Guru' because, after his father's death, he wore two **kirpans**

(swords). One sword represented spiritual power, and the other, worldly power. These two swords appeared on the flags of his army and are now on the Sikh flag, the **Nishan Sahib**.

Guru Har Gobind Ji trained Sikhs to fight in order to defend themselves.

Even today, some Sikhs in India still wear 'warrior uniform'.

Guru Har Rai Ji (1644–61)

Guru Har Rai Ji was fourteen years old when he became the seventh Guru. His father instructed him that he should always have 2200 soldiers and horses with him.

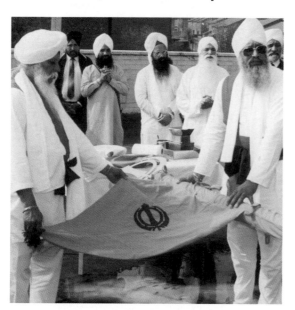

Sikhs holding the Nishan Sahib

Guru Har Rai Ji

Guru Har Rai Ji set up a system so that free medicines were given to those who were sick. Today, some **gurdwaras** in India still give free medical treatment to the poor.

The emperor of India asked Guru Har Rai Ji to explain his hymns. He sent his son, Ram Rai, instead, telling him that not one word of the hymns could be changed because they were the words of God. Ram Rai broke the rules which his father had given him and so Guru Har Rai Ji declared that the next Guru would be his youngest son, Har Krishan.

Guru Har Krishan Ji (1661–64)

Guru Har Krishan Ji was only five years old when he succeeded his father and he is sometimes called the 'Child Guru'. He died of smallpox at the age of eight and named his great uncle as his successor. Many people who had smallpox were healed when they drank spring water which he gave to them.

There is a famous gurdwara called Bangla Sahib at the site of Guru Har Krishan Ji's place of death in Delhi.

Guru Tegh Bahadur Ji (1664–75)

Guru Tegh Bahadur Ji was the youngest son of Guru Har Gobind Ji. His name means 'brave sword'.

Many people plotted against Guru Tegh Bahadur Ji. He fought against the Mogul rulers who were destroying Sikh temples and forcing people to convert to Islam. The emperor had made Sikhs and Hindus pay large taxes, and closed their schools and temples. Guru Tegh Bahadur Ji fought the emperor and was arrested.

Four of the Guru's companions were executed while he was made to watch. Then he was also killed.

Guru Tegh Bahadur Ji is respected as he died protecting the liberty of Sikhs and Hindus. A gurdwara called Sis Ganj Sahib stands in Delhi where he was executed.

Learning about religion

❶ a Why do two swords appear on the Sikh flag, the Nishan Sahib?

 b Explain one reason why Guru Har Rai Ji is remembered today.

❷ Why did Guru Har Rai Ji not choose his son to succeed him as Guru?

❸ Why is Guru Tegh Bahadur Ji regarded with such respect?

Learning from religion

❶ a What can we learn about obedience from the story of Ram Rai?

 b In what ways should people be obedient today?

❷ How important is it to stand up for freedom, as Guru Tegh Bahadur Ji did?

❸ What can we learn from the example of Guru Tegh Bahadur Ji about the way in which we treat people of other religions?

Guru Gobind Singh Ji

In this section you will:

● learn about the life and teachings of Guru Gobind Singh Ji

● consider what we can learn from his example and how it might influence people's lives.

Guru Gobind Singh Ji (1666–1708)

Guru Gobind Singh Ji was nine years old when his father, Guru Tegh Bahadur Ji, was executed. He was the last human Guru, and probably the most famous after **Guru Nanak Dev Ji**.

Guru Gobind Rai Ji, as he was originally known, was very clever at languages and a skilled horseman, archer and hunter. He was also a great poet, and a book of his poems called the **Dasam Granth** (the Tenth Collection) is second in importance to the **Guru Granth Sahib Ji** itself.

Guru Gobind Rai Ji is remembered for two very important contributions to **Sikhism**.

He formed the **Khalsa**, the 'community of the pure', and he chose the **Adi Granth**, now called the Guru Granth Sahib Ji, to succeed him and to be the final Guru.

In 1699 CE Sikhs from all over the Punjab were gathered at Anandpur Sahib, which is in a valley at the foot of the Himalayas. This was **Baisakhi**, the time of the Hindu festival of the wheat harvest which is celebrated on 13 April.

Guru Gobind Rai Ji gave a new meaning to Baisakhi for Sikhs.

He asked for five men to give their life for their faith. Each man went into a tent and the Guru then came out with blood on his sword. After the fifth man had gone inside, the tent was opened to show that all five were alive and well.

These men, the **panj piare** ('Five Beloved Ones') had been prepared to die for their faith. This event was the founding of the Khalsa – the community of the pure. From now on, all Sikhs were encouraged to wear the **panj kakke** – five Ks. Guru Gobind Rai Ji also said that all Sikh males should take the name **Singh** meaning 'lion'; and Sikh females should take the name **Kaur** which means 'princess'. He then changed his name to Guru Gobind Singh Ji. He dissolved sugar crystals in water and

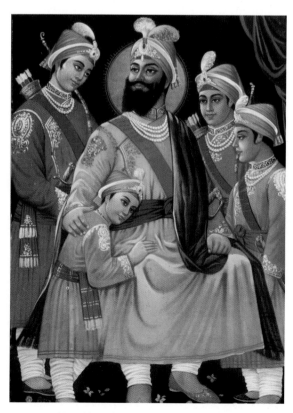

Guru Gobind Singh Ji with his sons

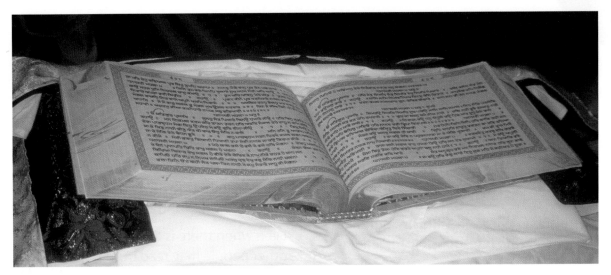

The Guru Granth Sahib Ji is the final Sikh Guru

stirred it with a **khanda** (a double-edged sword), then he sprinkled it over the panj piare.

The events at Baisakhi in 1699 CE marked the founding of the Khalsa and, since then, the festival of Baisakhi has been the beginning of the Sikh New Year.

Guru Gobind Singh Ji and his followers in Anandpur were under attack from the Mogul armies, and he and his wife had to leave. Many battles were fought between the Khalsa and the Moguls. During these battles, Guru Gobind Singh Ji lost his four sons and his mother. Countless numbers of Sikhs were killed, but more and more joined the ranks of the Khalsa.

Guru Gobind Singh Ji died of stab wounds in 1708 CE.

When he was dying, he took five coins and a coconut. He placed them in front of the Adi Granth. This was the way in which a new Guru was named, and so, by doing this, he was naming the Adi Granth as his successor. From then on, the Adi Granth was known as the Guru Granth Sahib Ji.

Learning about religion

❶ a What special skills did Guru Gobind Rai Ji have?

   b Explain one of the reasons that Guru Gobind Singh Ji is remembered today.

❷ Explain the importance of the panj piare.

❸ Why do you think that Guru Gobind Singh Ji chose the Guru Granth Sahib Ji to succeed him?

Learning from religion

❶ What can we learn about faith from the story of the panj piare?

❷ Explain why it might be important to stand up for your faith or beliefs.

❸ What can we learn from the example of Guru Gobind Singh Ji?

Sikh leaders

In this section you will:
- learn about leaders in Sikhism
- find out about the work of the granthi.

There are no priests in **Sikhism**, but there is a person who is responsible for leading the services.

Anyone who is a member of the **Khalsa** can read from the **Guru Granth Sahib Ji**, but it is usual for a **gurdwara** to have a person who is specially trained. This person is called a **granthi**, or 'reader', and can be a man or a woman.

The granthi also has to look after the Guru Granth Sahib Ji.

In some gurdwaras the granthi is employed full time and this is funded by the local community. In small villages in the Punjab, as elsewhere, most granthis are part time and have other jobs. In larger gurdwaras the granthis works for the gurdwara full time.

Even when there is a full-time granthi, other people may read from the Guru Granth Sahib Ji and may also lead the worship and the singing.

As well as being responsible for worship in the gurdwara, some granthis may visit the sick and needy and comfort those who are mourning a death. However, Sikhs believe that these duties also belong to the whole of the Sikh community.

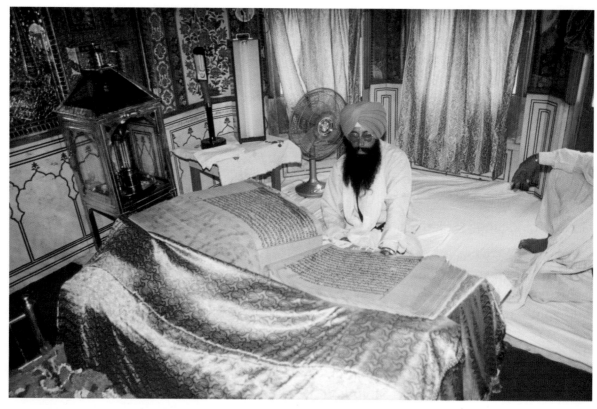

A granthi reading from the Guru Granth Sahib Ji

Ragis perform an important role in the gurdwara

As well as the granthi, a **ragi** is another important person in the gurdwara. During services a ragi sits to the side of the Guru Granth Sahib Ji and provides music for singing. The most common instruments are the baja, like a harmonium, and a tabla or jorri, which is a type of drum.

Learning about religion

❶ **a** What is a granthi?

b Explain the contribution a granthi makes to a Sikh community.

❷ **a** What are the different duties of a granthi?

b Why do Sikhs believe that these duties should be shared among the Sikh community?

❸ Why do you think ragis are important in a gurdwara?

Learning from religion

❶ Why might it be helpful if everyone could read from holy books?

❷ How might people look after one another in the community, in the same way that Sikhs do?

Sikh beliefs about God

In this section you will:
- learn what Sikhs believe about God
- consider how the Mool Mantar is important.

The Mool Mantar

One of the central statements of Sikh belief is in a hymn called the **Mool Mantar**.

Mool Mantar means 'basic teaching' and it is found at the beginning of the **Guru Granth Sahib Ji**.

It is repeated each day during early morning prayer.

The first words of the Mool Mantar are **Ik Onkar** meaning 'There is one God'.

The Mool Mantar

The symbol for Ik Onkar is seen in many places, such as badges, on the walls of a **gurdwara** and in the home. It is a constant reminder to Sikhs of their faith and belief in **Waheguru**.

Beliefs about God

The most important belief in **Sikhism** is that there is only one God – Waheguru. God is beyond the understanding of human beings. God cannot be described because humans can only describe God in human terms which will always be less than what God is. God is neither male nor female. God is the creator who created the world for people to use and enjoy. God is everywhere and beyond everything. God created people, and taught them the difference between right and wrong.

The Mool Mantar

Ik Onkar	There is only one God
Sat Nam	Eternal truth is God's name
Karta Purakh	God is the creator
Nir Bhau	God is without fear
Nir Vair	God is without hate
Akal Murat	Immortal, without form
Ajuni	Beyond birth and death
Saibhang	God is the enlightener
Gur Parshad	God can be reached through the mercy and grace of the true **Guru**

Although people know the difference between what is right and what is wrong, they still have to choose for themselves which path they will follow. God is present in everyone's soul, but can only be seen by those who are blessed. God is personal and is available to everyone.

Sikhs believe that the one God is the God of all religions. No one religion can claim to be the only true way to God and different religions are just different ways towards God. Therefore it is not important which God people worship. What is important is that they follow the teachings of God so that they have the chance of achieving **mukti**, or escape from rebirth.

You are Father, Mother, Friend, Brother, with you as support everywhere, what fear can I have?

Guru Granth Sahib Ji

There are many names for God, such as:

Sat Nam	Eternal Reality
Akal Purakh	Eternal One
Waheguru	Wonderful Lord

Learning about religion

❶ a What does the Mool Mantar tell us about God?

 b Explain why this prayer is so important.

❷ What do you think Sikhs mean when they say that there is only one God for all religions?

Learning from religion

❶ a What can we learn about God from Sikh teaching?

 b In what ways might this belief help other people?

❷ Carefully think about how you might describe God. Write down your thoughts and try and explain your description.

One very important Sikh belief is that Sikhs should keep the name of God in their minds and live their lives as God would wish.

Ik Onkar – the first words of the Mool Mantar

Sikh beliefs about life

In this section you will:

● learn what Sikhs believe about how they should try and live their lives

● find out about mukti.

Sikhs believe that everything that happens is **Hukam** – the will of God.

There is a part of God in each person and this soul is taken back to God when a person is finally released from the cycle of rebirth.

Sikhs believe that there are nearly eight and a half million different forms of life and that many souls have to be reborn through a large number of these before they can finally reach God. Each time something dies the soul is reborn. It is only humans who can know the difference between right and wrong and so it is only when the soul is in a human being that the cycle can be broken.

Karma – actions and their consequences – decide whether a soul can be set loose from the cycle. Freedom from this cycle is called **mukti**.

There are several things that can stop a soul reaching mukti:

● **a hankar** – pride

● **kam** – lust or desire

● **karodh** – anger

● **lobh** – greed

● **moh** – being too attached to the world

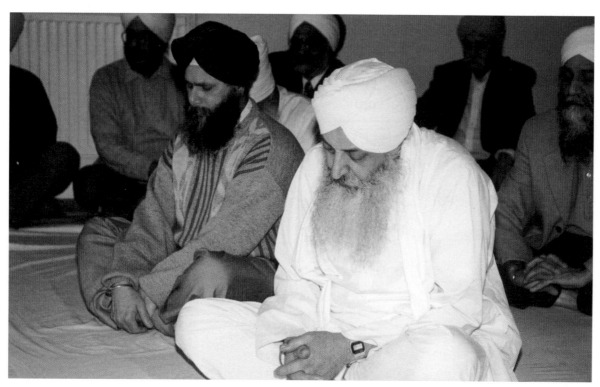

Prayer is an important part of Sikh worship

Sikhs believe in hard work and helping others

- **Manmukh** – being self-centred instead of God-centred (**gurmukh**)

- **Maya** – delusion, that is looking at the world and ignoring God.

Those who live without these devote their life to **sewa** – selfless service to others.

In order to avoid these dangers Sikhs are encouraged to follow these rules of conduct:

- There is only one God. Worship and pray to God alone, and remember God at all times.

- Always work hard, and share with others.

- Live a truthful life.

- Remember that men and women are equal in God's eyes.

- The whole human race is one. All distinctions are wrong.

- Idols, magic, omens, fasts, marks on the face and sacred threads are banned.

- Dress simply and modestly.

- **Khalsa** Sikh women should not wear the veil. Neither women nor men should make holes in their ears or noses.

- Live a married life.

- Put your faith in the **Guru Granth Sahib Ji.**

- Avoid lust, anger, greed, attachment to worldly things and arrogance.

- Live a humble and simple life.

Learning about religion

❶ a What is Hukam?

   b What do Sikhs mean by karma?

❷ a Explain why mukti is so important.

   b Explain what can stop a soul from reaching mukti.

Learning from religion

❶ a What can we learn about a way of life from Sikh teaching?

   b How might this belief help other people?

❷ Why might it be important to have a code of conduct?

❸ What rules of conduct would you include in a code of conduct for your community?

Signs and symbols 1

In this section you will:
- begin to learn what the five Ks mean, and how they are symbolized
- consider how wearing the five Ks affects Sikhs' lives.

Kara

Symbols are a way in which we remind ourselves, and other people, of important ideas and beliefs. Signs and symbols are used in everyday life and many religions have particular symbols of their own. Sikhism has many important symbols.

The five Ks

Sikhs who are members of the **Khalsa** (the community of the pure) have to wear five symbols; **kara, kangha, kesh, kachera** and **kirpan**. These **five Ks – panj kakke** – show that the person is a Sikh. They also have spiritual meanings and are symbols of the faith. They come from the establishment of the Khalsa by **Guru** Gobind Singh Ji at **Baisakhi** in 1699 CE and remind Sikhs of their beliefs and their history.

Kangha

The **kangha** is a comb used by Sikhs to keep their hair clean and tidy. Guru Gobind Singh Ji said that cleanliness was very important. Sikhs are encouraged to wash their hair early each morning. They then comb it and wind it into a topknot. The kangha is placed in the topknot to keep it in place. Sometimes the kangha has a small image of a **kirpan** (sword) on it. Using the khanga to keep their hair in place also reminds Sikhs of the need for discipline in order to live according to God's will.

Kara

The **kara** is a bracelet, made of iron or steel, and worn on the right wrist. Some Sikhs wear two karas. The metal represents strength, and the circle is a symbol of unity and eternity which has no beginning and no end. This shows the Sikh view of God who is eternal and infinite. The circle also stands for the unity between Sikhs and between Sikhs and God.

Kangha

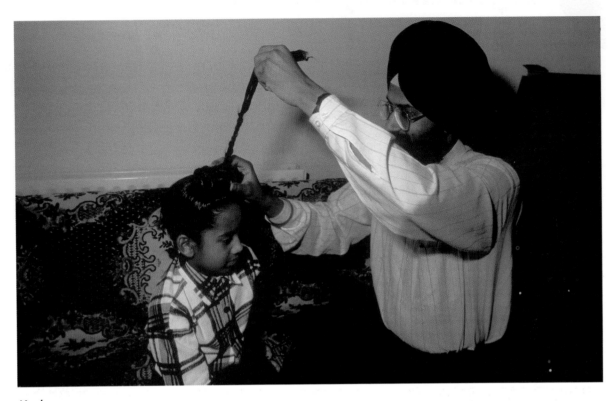

Kesh

Kesh

Kesh is uncut hair. Khalsa Sikhs do not cut their hair. Guru Gobind Singh Ji said that hair should be allowed to grow as God intended it to. Many Sikh men keep their hair covered with a **turban**, but this is not one of the five Ks. Some women also wear a turban. Young boys may wear a cloth over their topknot to keep their hair clean.

Learning about religion

❶ What does a kara mean to Sikhs?

❷ **a** What is special about kesh?

b Why do you think Sikhs insist on their right to wear a turban?

❸ Search the Internet (or use a CD-ROM) to find information about times when Sikhs have not been allowed to wear their turbans in Britain (try www.sikhism.org.uk/main.htm to begin with). Write down your findings.

Learning from religion

❶ **a** What do the five Ks teach us about how we might live our lives?

b Do you think it might help people to wear symbols of their faith?

❷ What other faith symbols can you think of?

❸ What symbols would you like to wear to say something about your way of life and beliefs?

Signs and symbols 2

In this section you will:

- learn about the kachera and kirpan and other Sikh symbols and think about the importance of these symbols
- consider how symbols are used in Sikhism and what can be learnt from this.

Kachera

Kachera are short trousers that are usually worn as undergarments. They are worn by both men and women. **Guru** Gobind

Singh Ji said that Sikhs should wear these short trousers as part of the **Khalsa** uniform. Hindus usually wore dhotis (a long loin cloth) or long cloaks. Both of these garments were unsuitable for fighting in and the kachera may have made it easier for Sikhs to fight in a battle if they had to.

Wearing these clothes reminds Sikhs that they must always be prepared to defend their religion and the rights of other people to practise their own faith. Today, these short trousers are seen as a symbol of modesty for many Sikhs and remind them of the need to live a good life according to the teachings of the Gurus.

Kachera, kangha, kara and kirpan

Kirpan

The **kirpan** is a sword worn by members of the Khalsa. The kirpan is a reminder of the courage of the first five Sikhs, the **panj piare**, who were willing to let Guru Gobind Singh Ji cut off their heads with a kirpan for the sake of their religion. So it is a symbol of bravery and of faith in God.

The kirpan is worn as a symbol of the Sikh being willing to defend his or her faith, or to defend the weak or oppressed.

Taking the kirpan out of its sheath would be considered disrespectful by some Sikhs. The kirpan is worn on a belt that goes across the shoulder under a coat. Because the kirpan is seen as a weapon, Sikhs outside of the Punjab have sometimes been told that they are not allowed to wear it in public. They have objected to the kirpan being called a dagger or a knife because it suggests that they are carrying it as a weapon. Sometimes the kirpan is worn as a very small symbol on the **kangha**.

Nishan Sahib

The Sikh flag and symbol is called the **Nishan Sahib**. This flag always flies outside a **gurdwara**. It is a triangle of saffron or orange cloth. On the flag is the **khanda**. The khanda itself has three important symbols on it. The first is a double-edged sword (itself known as a khanda), which is used to stir **amrit** in gurdwara services. The second is the **kara** (circular bangle) given to Sikhs as a symbol of their unity and oneness with God. The third is two kirpans. The two kirpans represent spiritual power and

worldly power and were first earned by Guru Har Gobind Ji.

The flag is treated with great respect and is renewed each year at the festival of **Baisakhi**.

Ik Onkar

The first words of the **Mool Mantar** are **Ik Onkar** meaning 'There is only one God'. The symbol for Ik Onkar is seen in many places, such as badges, on the walls of a gurdwara and in the home.

Learning about religion

❶ a What are the panj kakke?

   b Explain why they are so important to Sikhs.

❷ What is special about the kirpan?

❸ Search the Internet for information about the five Ks (try www.sikhism.org.uk/main.htm to begin with). Write a report about what you find.

Learning from religion

❶ Why do you think it would be helpful to have a symbol like the Ik Onkar?

❷ What symbols do you see in daily life?

❸ Why is it sometimes easier to say something using symbols rather than words?

The gurdwara

In this section you will:
- learn about the gurdwara
- think about their importance
- consider how worship in a gurdwara affects people's lives.

Gurdwara means 'the doorway of the **Guru**'. It is a building in which the Sikh holy book, the **Guru Granth Sahib Ji**, is kept, and it is a place where Sikhs worship together. A gurdwara is also a community centre for Sikhs.

Outside a gurdwara there are usually symbols which show what it is. There will be a flagpole flying the **Nishan Sahib**, the Sikh flag. This is triangular, orange or saffron in colour and on it is a symbol known as the **khanda**. This consists of two curved **kirpans** (swords), a khanda (double-edged sword) and a **kara** (circular bangle).

Shoes must not be worn in the main prayer hall of a gurdwara. There are also sinks so that people can wash their hands before worship, and a box of head coverings as people must cover their heads as a sign of respect. Anyone is welcome in a gurdwara as long as they have no traces of alcohol or tobacco on them.

In the main prayer hall there is a large carpeted area. There are no seats or chairs because the **sadhsangat** (congregation) sit cross-legged on the floor. Feet must not point towards the Guru Granth Sahib Ji. Women and men sometimes sit on opposite sides of the gurdwara so they do not distract each other during worship.

Sikhs in a gurdwara – the central place of Sikh community worship

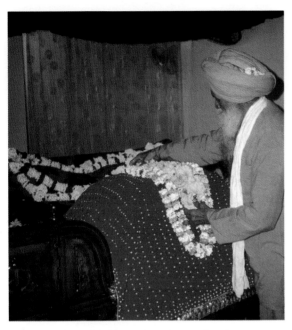

The Guru Granth Sahib Ji being laid to rest for the night

At one end of the hall is the **manji** or sahib (a raised platform) with a **chanani** (canopy). There are cushions on the manji with **romalla** (beautiful cloths) draped over them. The romalla covers the Guru Granth Sahib Ji when it is not being read. The **granthi**, who may be a man or a woman, sits behind the Guru Granth Sahib Ji, facing the worshippers.

In front of the manji there is a long box called a **golak**, in which worshippers place their money offerings.

On another platform, the **ragis** (musicians) sit to play their instruments during **kirtan** (hymn singing). Music is an important aspect of Sikh worship. Verses from the scriptures are set to music and called **shabads**. The singing of shabads is called kirtan. The hymns found in the Guru Granth Sahib Ji are known as **Gurbani** which means 'the words of the Guru'.

It is important for Sikhs to remember the words of the shabads. Before a hymn is sung the ragis will read it and say a few words of explanation.

Inside a gurdwara there is a room which is the rest room for the holy scriptures. The rest room has a bed, with pillows, covers and a canopy. The Guru Granth Sahib Ji is 'put to bed' each night by the granthi or another Sikh who says the prayer, **Kirtan Sohila**. Each morning it is 'woken up' and placed on the manji.

Learning about religion

❶ Write down the main features of a gurdwara.

❷ **a** What is the importance of the sinks and the box of head coverings?

   b Explain how people sit in a gurdwara.

❸ Why do you think it is important for Sikhs to understand the shabads?

Learning from religion

❶ **a** What might people learn about respect from the way in which Sikhs prepare to enter the prayer hall?

   b List the good points and bad points of men and women sitting together when they pray.

❷ What might people learn about worship from seeing Sikhs in a gurdwara?

The langar

In this section you will:

- learn about the langar
- think about how the sharing of food might affect peoples lives
- consider the importance of sharing and equality in Sikhism.

Every **gurdwara** has a **langar** – 'Guru's kitchen' or eating area. The meal eaten here is also called a langar. The langar is part of worship and a very important aspect of Sikh life. There is no charge for the food served in the langar.

Guru Nanak Dev Ji set up the langar because he rejected the Hindu **caste** system where people of different castes are not allowed to eat together. Guru Nanak Dev Ji wanted to stress the idea that everyone is equal, so he wanted everyone to be able to eat the same food in the langar. Also, everyone was to share the tasks of preparation, cooking, serving and cleaning. This shows **sewa** – selfless service to others in the **sadhsangat** (community), to the gurdwara and to the world outside, and is a very important aspect of **Sikhism**.

This teaching was continued by Guru Amar Das Ji. He made a rule that no one could see him until they had first eaten in the langar.

Sikh families consider it a privilege to provide for the langar and to serve others. There is usually a waiting list of people who want to provide the langar each week.

Members of the sadhsangat (congregation) are served their food and sit in rows, on the

Sharing food together in the langar illustrates the equality of all people before God

Vegetarian food is served in the langar so as not to exclude anyone

floor or at long tables with benches. Food is usually served by the male members of the congregation. There are no special places and everyone eats the same food.

Although not all Sikhs are vegetarian, no meat is served in the langar so that no one will be excluded from the meal. Sikhs are not allowed to eat any meat which has been ritually slaughtered.

Learning about religion

❶ a What do you understand by the word 'langar'?

b Explain Guru Nanak Dev Ji's teaching about the langar.

❷ a Why do you think Guru Amar Das Ji refused to see anyone until they had eaten in the langar?

b Explain how food is prepared and served in the langar.

❸ Why do you think the langar is so important to Sikhism?

Learning from religion

❶ Why might other people set up places which are similar to the langar?

❷ Think of examples of ways in which people suffer as a result of discrimination, and write about them.

❸ What might people learn about sharing and equality from the idea of the langar?

Worship 1

In this section you will:

● learn about the Sikh service of worship

● consider how regular worship might affect people's lives.

There is no special day for Sikhs to worship, although Sunday is popular because it is a day when most people do not go to work. Some communities have their services daily or in the evenings.

Prayers are said every morning and evening in the **gurdwara**, but not all members of the local community attend these.

Congregational worship is called **diwan** or **kirtan**, which means hymn singing, because verses from the **Guru Granth Sahib Ji** are sung as part of the service.

The weekly service

After bathing, members of the **sadhsangat** (congregation) remove their shoes, cover their heads and wash their hands before entering the prayer hall.

Sikhs approach the **manji** or **sahib** (platform) on which the Guru Granth Sahib Ji is placed. They kneel on their hands and knees and lower their heads until their foreheads touch the floor as a sign of respect.

Then they make an offering of money, flowers or food for the use of the Sikh community.

Sikhs may then greet other members of the congregation by saying **Waheguru** before sitting cross-legged on the floor facing the manji. Men and women usually sit on opposite sides of the prayer hall.

The service may last for two hours or more.

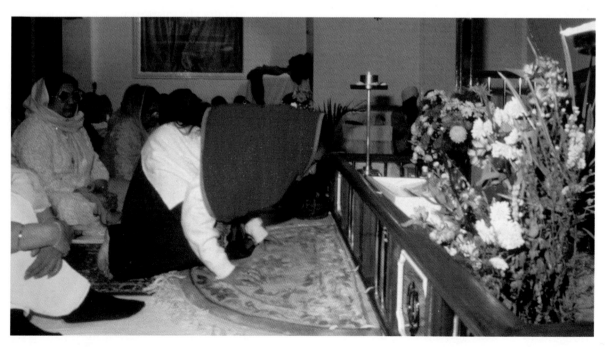

Sikhs kneeling in front of the Guru Granth Sahib Ji

The Ardas is an important Sikh prayer

It begins early in the morning when the Guru Granth Sahib Ji is removed from its resting place and placed on the manji. There are readings from the Guru Granth Sahib Ji until the **ragis** (musicians) arrive. The readings are chosen at random.

People chant verses from the Guru Granth Sahib Ji and the ragis sing and accompany them on musical instruments. The congregation joins in the hymns. This part of the service is called kirtan.

A sermon is given by a member of the Sikh community. This is usually an explanation of the readings from the Guru Granth Sahib Ji.

At the end of the service, there are prayers which include six verses from **Anand Sahib**, a hymn written by Guru Amar Das Ji, the last part of the **Japji Sahib**, written by **Guru Nanak Dev Ji**, a verse from a hymn by Guru Arjan Dev Ji, and, finally, **Ardas**.

The congregation face the Guru Granth Sahib Ji with their hands together.

The first part of Ardas mentions God and all the Gurus. The second part reminds Sikhs that the Guru Granth Sahib Ji is God's word, and of the faithful Sikhs of the past. The final part of Ardas is a prayer asking God to keep the **Khalsa** faithful and for the well-being of people of all races and religions.

While Ardas is being said the **karah parshad** (a sweet food that is shared by the congregation) is prepared, by stirring it with a **kirpan**. After Ardas, everyone sits down. The karah parshad is offered first to five practising Sikhs, in memory of the **panj piare**, and then handed out to everyone present. This shared food shows that everyone is equal before God.

Learning about religion

❶ Explain what Sikhs do when they enter the gurdwara.

❷ a Why are the offerings that Sikhs make in the prayer hall important?

   b What is special about Ardas?

❸ How is respect shown to the Guru Granth Sahib Ji during the service?

Learning from religion

❶ How do you think it might help non-religious people if they were to learn about and show respect for holy books?

❷ Find out how some other religions treat their holy books and why.

❸ Explain how non-Sikhs might learn from the teaching in the final part of Ardas.

Worship 2

Nam Simran

Guru Nanak Dev Ji taught that the most important form of worship is **bhakti** (devotion to God). Some people say that the whole of **Sikhism** is bhakti.

When Sikhs meditate on, or think about, the name of God this is known as **Nam Simran** (thinking of the name). People sense God and grow ever closer to God.

Sikhs remember the presence of God through **Nam Japna**, repeating the name of God, **Waheguru**. This can be said aloud or silently.

Morning prayer

After bathing, meditate upon the Lord and your body and mind will become pure.

Guru Granth Sahib Ji

Guru Ram Das Ji said:

He who calls himself a Sikh of the great Sat Guru should rise early and meditate on God's name.

Guru Granth Sahib Ji

Mala – prayer beads

Sikhs get up early each day to pray and meditate. This is called **amritvela**. The early morning is peaceful and a good time for prayer and meditation. First, they take a bath, and get dressed. Then, after covering their heads, they can begin prayer.

Prayer begins with the **Japji Sahib**, a hymn of 38 verses which comes from the first section of the **Guru Granth Sahib Ji**. The opening verses of the Japji Sahib are the **Mool Mantar**. After the Japji Sahib, other prayers are said and some Sikhs will read hymns from a collection called the Gutka. At the end of prayers, Sikhs meditate. Some people use **mala** (prayer beads) to help them.

Prayers must not be said while doing other things and, ideally, should be done in a quiet place where there are no distractions.

Throughout the day, some Sikhs will often practise Nam Japna this is done by repeating the word 'Waheguru' under their breath.

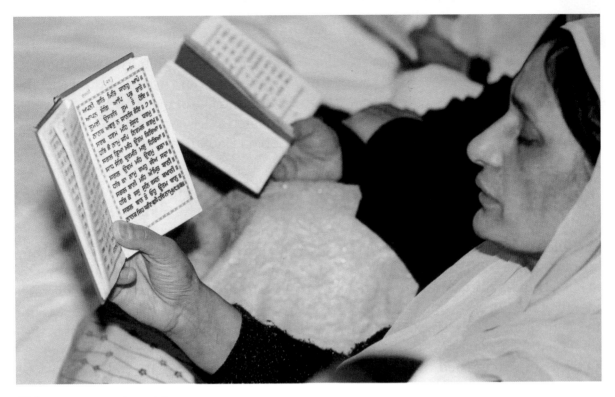

Sikh women praying at home

Evening prayer

In the evening there are set hymns and prayers. **Sodar Rahiras** is said before the evening meal. Just before going to bed Sikhs will recite a small group of hymns called the **Kirtan Sohila**.

Learning about religion

❶ a Write down what you understand by the word 'bhakti'.

b Explain what is meant by Nam Simran.

❷ Read the two quotes from the Guru Granth Sahib Ji. What do they tell you about Sikh prayer?

❸ What conditions are important for prayer?

Learning from religion

❶ a What can we learn about prayer from the daily prayers of Sikhs?

b Do you think it might help people of other faiths if they were to pray more regularly? Would it help you?

❷ Find out about different ways in which people meditate.

The Guru Granth Sahib Ji

The **Guru Granth Sahib Ji** is the holy scripture of the Sikhs. The book is written in Punjabi using the **Gurmukhi** – 'from the mouth of the **Guru**' – script. Every copy of the Guru Granth Sahib Ji is exactly the same, with 1430 pages. The Guru Granth Sahib Ji can be translated, but these translations are not used in Sikh worship.

The Guru Granth Sahib Ji is a collection of the teachings and hymns of **Guru Nanak Dev Ji** and five of the other Sikh Gurus. It is treated as a living Guru by Sikhs, as Guru Gobind Singh Ji taught.

The second Guru, Guru Angad Dev Ji, wrote down the hymns of Guru Nanak Dev Ji. The third Guru, Guru Amar Das Ji, composed more hymns, including the **Anand Sahib** (Hymn of Bliss). The fourth Guru, Guru Ram Das Ji, composed the **Lavan**, the four verses which are sung at a wedding ceremony. The fourth Guru, Guru Arjan Dev Ji, brought all the hymns of the other Gurus into one single set of scriptures, known as the **Adi Granth**.

The Guru Granth Sahib Ji has 1430 pages of scripture

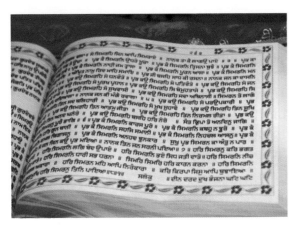

A page of the Guru Granth Sahib Ji written in Gurmukhi script

Guru Gobind Singh Ji added more hymns written by his father, Guru Tegh Bahadur Ji. He announced that, after his death, there would be no other living Guru, but that the scriptures should now become the Guru.

The Adi Granth then became a 'Guru' and was known as the Guru Granth Sahib Ji.

The Guru Granth Sahib Ji is given the same respect that was shown to the human Gurus during their lifetimes. It has a special resting place where it is put to bed every evening.

At the beginning of each day, the **granthi**, and any other Sikhs present, form a procession to carry the Guru Granth Sahib Ji to its position in the main prayer hall of the **gurdwara**.

The Guru Granth Sahib Ji is never placed on the ground and Sikhs never turn their back on it.

While the Guru Granth Sahib Ji is being read, the granthi waves a special fan, called a **chauri**, over the pages of the book. This chauri has a long handle and is made from yak hair. It remembers the **pakha,** which was used by Sikhs walking with the Gurus to keep them cool in the hot areas of the Punjab.

The Guru Granth Sahib Ji is of very great importance for Sikhs, who believe that it is **Gurbani** or the word of God.

Many Sikhs own a copy of the Guru Granth Sahib Ji and take care to show it respect.

Some Sikh families have a copy of the **Dasam Granth** (poetry written by Guru Gobind Singh Ji and not included in the Guru Granth Sahib Ji) or the sacred **Nit nem** (a prayer book) at home.

Learning about religion

❶ a   What do you understand by the word 'Gurmukhi'?

  b   How did the Guru Granth Sahib Ji come into being?

❷ a   Why do you think the use of the chauri is important?

  b   Explain how the Guru Granth Sahib Ji is shown respect in the gurdwara.

Learning from religion

❶   What might people learn from the respect which Sikhs show to the Guru Granth Sahib Ji?

❷   Do you think a book can show the actual words of God? Explain your views.

❸   What things do some people show respect to in their lives?

Festivals 1

In this section you will:

● learn about Sikh festivals and how these are celebrated

● consider why celebrating these festivals is important to Sikhs.

There are two different types of festivals in **Sikhism**:

● Special holy days which celebrate events in the lives of the **Gurus**. These are known as **gurpurbs** – Gurus' remembrance days.

● Other celebrations are held on the same days as some Hindu festivals. These are known as **melas**.

Gurpurbs

The gurpurbs are days that remember the births and deaths of the Gurus. Some of these are particularly important. They include:

● the martyrdom of Guru Arjan Dev Ji (May/June) (16 June)

● the installation of the **Guru Granth Sahib Ji** (August/early September)

● the birthday of **Guru Nanak Dev Ji** (November)

● the birthday of Guru Gobind Singh Ji (December) (5 January)

● the martyrdom of Guru Tegh Bahadur Ji (December) (24 November).

Part of the celebration of a gurpurb is a complete reading of the Guru Granth Sahib Ji. This is called the **Akhand Path**.

The Guru Granth Sahib Ji being carried through the streets at a gurpurb

Sikhs celebrating the birthday of Guru Nanak Dev Ji

Sikhs usually come to the **gurdwara** on the last day to hear the last pages of the Guru Granth Sahib Ji being read.

In India, these events are celebrated on the actual day, but in other countries, they are usually celebrated on the closest Sunday. The Akhand Path begins on Friday and ends at the Sunday service.

In India, the Guru Granth Sahib Ji is traditionally carried through the streets in a procession with five men representing the **panj piare**.

Learning about religion

❶ a What is a gurpurb?

b Why are certain days celebrated as gurpurbs?

❷ Why is the Akhand Path a sign of great respect to the Gurus?

❸ Visit The Sikhism Homepage on the Internet (www.sikhs.org) and find out more about the celebration of gurpurbs. You could also try www.theresite.org.uk/.

Learning from religion

❶ What might people learn from the way in which Sikhs celebrate gurpurbs?

❷ 'Although it's a good idea to celebrate birthdays, it is strange to celebrate someone's death.' What do you think?

❸ Do you think that reading a holy book, as Sikhs do during the Akhand Path, might be a good way to celebrate festivals?

Festivals 2

In this section you will:
- learn more about how Sikh festivals are celebrated
- consider why these are important to Sikhs.

Changing the Nishan Sahib at Baisakhi

Mela

There are three major Sikh festivals which are held on the same day as Hindu festivals. They are:

- **Baisakhi**
- **Divali Mela**
- **Hola Mohalla Mela**.

The word **mela** means a fair.

Guru Amar Das Ji said that Sikhs should come together for worship during Baisakhi and Divali Mela, and Guru Gobind Singh Ji added Hola Mohalla Mela. Celebrating these festivals showed that Sikhs were a separate religious group and that they no longer celebrated the festivals as Hindus do.

Baisakhi

Baisakhi is the month of the wheat harvest in the Punjab. The festival is on 13 April and marks the Sikh New Year.

In 1699 CE Guru Gobind Singh Ji founded the **Khalsa** at Baisakhi. Sikhs also remember 1919 CE when 400 Sikhs (many of them women and children) were killed by British soldiers who had been ordered to stop their Baisakhi celebrations at Jallianwala Bagh in **Amritsar**.

The **Nishan Sahib** (Sikh flag) is changed at Baisakhi. During the festival, the **Akhand Path** is read and initiation ceremonies (**Amrit**) are held.

Divali Mela

Divali Mela is celebrated throughout India in the autumn, and marks the end of the rainy season.

Sikhs remember the story of Guru Har Gobind Ji who returned to Amritsar on Divali. He had been in prison while the Mogul emperor, Jehangir, tried to stop the growth of **Sikhism**. The emperor was sick and his doctors said he could only be cured if he released the Guru. Guru Har Gobind Ji was released, but said that he would not go unless he could take 52 Hindu princes who were also in prison with him.

Jehangir told the Guru that he would free as many princes as could hold on to his clothes as he walked through a narrow passage. Guru Har Gobind Ji made himself a coat with long tassels, and all the princes went with him.

The Golden Temple during the festival of Divali Mela

Many Sikh homes are decorated with divas (clay lamps), candles and coloured lights. There are special meals and firework displays. It is a time of rejoicing. People give sweets to their friends and relatives. Services are held in **gurdwaras** and the Golden Temple in Amritsar is lit up.

Hola Mohalla Mela

In 1700 CE Guru Gobind Singh Ji held a three-day festival at **Anandpur Sahib**. This became a time for Sikhs to train as soldiers.

Hola Mohalla means 'attack and counter-attack'.

Learning about religion

❶ a What is a mela?

 b Why did Guru Amar Das Ji want Sikhs to come together at these festivals?

❷ What is remembered at Baisakhi?

❸ Which of the three festivals do you think is the most important, Why?

Learning from religion

❶ What might people learn from the way in which Sikhs celebrate the melas?

❷ Why do you think festivals are important in all religions?

❸ Think about ways in which people could follow the example of Guru Har Gobind Ji?

Pilgrimage 1

There are no special times for pilgrimage in **Sikhism**. Many Sikhs try to visit the places associated with their religion. Sikhs believe that God is everywhere, and so no one place is more holy than another.

The **Gurus** taught that it was not important to make special journeys to visit holy places.

True pilgrimage consists of the contemplation of the name of God and the cultivation of inner knowledge.

Guru Granth Sahib Ji

There is no place of pilgrimage equal to the Gurus. The Guru alone is the pool of contentment. The Guru is the river from which pure water is obtained, by which the dirt of evil understanding is washed away.

Guru Granth Sahib Ji

The Punjab in India is the homeland of Sikhs and more than half of the people who live there are Sikhs and speak Punjabi. Of the world population of more than 19 million Sikhs, 80 per cent live in the Punjab. Other Sikhs may also visit the Golden Temple at **Amritsar** and places

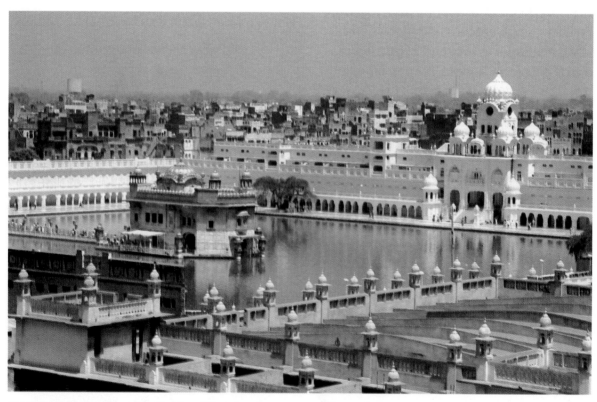

Harimandir Sahib – the Golden Temple – is a very important centre of pilgrimage for Sikhs

which are associated with the Gurus and their lives. These visits are called **yatras**.

The Harimandir Sahib

The most popular place to go on a yatra is the **Harimandir Sahib** – the Golden Temple at Amritsar. Harimandir means God's House.

The Harimandir Sahib is a very special **gurdwara**. The first Guru, **Guru Nanak Dev Ji**, chose the site and said that the fourth Guru would build there. Guru Ram Das Ji began to build a large pool there, which he filled with **amrit** (nectar), and named it Amritsar. This sort of pool is called a **serovar**. His son, Guru Arjan Dev Ji, built the Harimandir Sahib on an island in the middle of the serovar in 1601 CE.

The Harimandir Sahib has always been a major meeting place for Sikhs. The Mogul emperors destroyed the temple and filled in the serovar. In 1740 CE the temple was used as a hall for dancing and drinking. Two Sikhs travelled from the south of India to kill the ruler of Amritsar and to restore the temple.

The dome and the upper walls of the Harimandir Sahib are covered in gold leaf. There is a door on each of the four walls to show that the Harimandir Sahib is open to everyone. A long marble walkway crosses the serovar to the west door of the Harimandir Sahib, while a wide promenade called the Pakirama runs round the pool. There are also rows of rooms where pilgrims can rest. The **langar** in the Harimandir Sahib is open every day and anyone can eat there. The langar provides daily food for many of the poor people of Amritsar.

Learning about religion

❶ a What is a yatra?

b Why might Sikhs visit Amritsar?

❷ What happens in the Harimandir Sahib?

❸ Create a poster to show the most important features of the Harimandir Sahib. Search the Internet to find pictures, and label them to explain why they are significant.

Learning from religion

❶ Think about the Sikh teaching that no place is more important than another because God is everywhere. What might people learn from this?

❷ Why do you think so many people feel that making a pilgrimage is important?

❸ Where you would like to go on a pilgrimage and why? How might it affect you?

Pilgrimage 2

In this section you will:

● learn about why Sikhs may visit other places of pilgrimage

● consider how pilgrimage might affect people's lives.

Akal Takht

Akal Takht means 'the Throne of the Eternal'. The Akal Takht faces the Golden Temple and was built by **Guru** Har Gobind Ji in 1609 CE. The building is used by Sikhs for political meetings and is the meeting place of the **Khalsa**. The highest Sikh court meets at the Akal Takht.

The Akal Takht houses the most sacred copy of the **Guru Granth Sahib Ji**. Each day, at 5 am in winter and 4 am in summer, it is carried in a golden carriage to the **Harimandir Sahib**. It is carried back to rest at 10 pm in winter and 11 pm in summer. Outside the building are two large flagpoles. One has the flag of Miri – temporal (earthly) authority, and the other of Piri – spiritual authority.

Anandpur Sahib

Anandpur Sahib is another special place for Sikhs. It is in a valley at the foot of the Himalayas. The ashes of the head of Guru Tegh Bahadur Ji are buried there and it is also the place where Guru Gobind Singh Ji founded the Khalsa. The most important celebrations for the festival of **Hola Mohalla Mela** take place at Anandpur.

Goindwal

Guru Amar Das Ji had a very deep well, or baoli, built at **Goindwal**. It provided safe drinking water and was surrounded by trees to improve the environment. It became a tradition for people to bathe in the well. People say the **Japji Sahib** on each of the 84 steps. Some people say that, by doing this, they will get nearer to **mukti**.

Pilgrimage, austerity [living simply], mercy, almsgiving and charity bring merit, be it as little as a mustard seed, but those who hear, believe and cherish the word, an inner pilgrimage and cleansing is theirs.

From the Japji Sahib

The Gurus said that ceremonial bathing served no purpose. When people recite the Japji Sahib going down into the well, they do not benefit from the bathing but because they have meditated on God's name.

If someone goes to bathe at a place of pilgrimage with the mind of a crook and the body of a thief then his outside will have been washed but his inside will be dirty twice over … The saints are good even without such washing. The thief remains a thief even if they bathe at a place of pilgrimage.

Guru Granth Sahib Ji

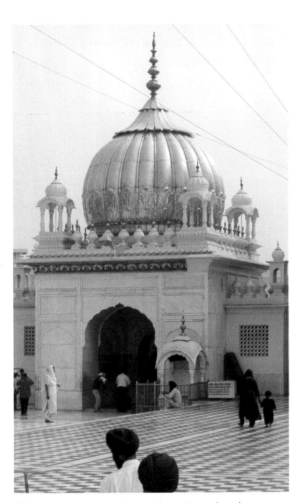

The entrance to the well at Goindwal

Learning about religion

❶ a   What is a baoli?

   b   Why might Sikhs visit Anandpur Sahib?

❷   Why is the Akal Takht important for Sikhs?

❸   What did the Gurus teach about pilgrimage and ritual bathing?

Learning from religion

❶ a   What might people learn from the Sikh teaching that how you live is more important than where you go or what you do there?

   b   The Akal Takht is a political, religious and community building. How might other religions benefit from a building like this?

❷   Design a flag using what you think are important symbols.

❸   Find out about pilgrimage in other religions and explain which style of pilgrimage you might find most useful.

Growing up

Birth

As soon as a baby is born, many Sikhs whisper the words of the **Mool Mantar** in its ear and place a drop of honey on its tongue.

The name-giving ceremony

Once the mother and child are well enough to go out, there is a special ceremony held at the **gurdwara**.

The **granthi** opens the **Guru Granth Sahib Ji** at random. The baby's name will begin with the first letter of the first hymn on the left-hand side of the page. The parents are then given some time to choose a name. This name is announced by the granthi who adds the title **Singh** for a boy or **Kaur** for a girl. The granthi then shouts 'Jo bole so nihal' (Whoever believes in the Truth will be saved) and the congregation reply 'Sat sri akahl' (The Truth is eternal).

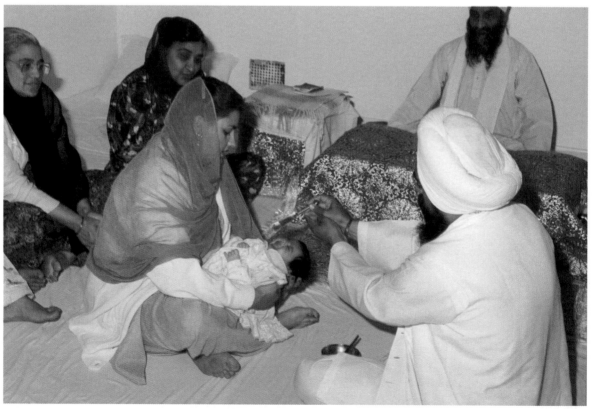

The name-giving ceremony is a special occasion, which takes place in the gurdwara

Hymns are sung from the Guru Granth Sahib Ji and the candidates drink the amrit. These words are said: 'The Khalsa is of God, the victory is to God.' The amrit is sprinkled on the hair and eyes of the candidates five times, and then the Mool Mantar is read. **Ardas** is said and karah parshad distributed to everyone.

Sikhs who do not join the Khalsa are called **Sahaj-dhari** – 'seekers after God'.

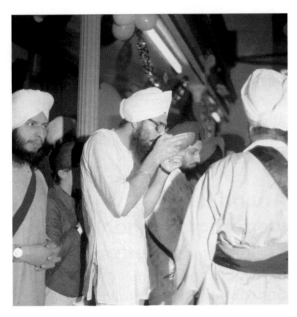

The Amrit ceremony is the initiation ceremony for Khalsa Sikhs

The ceremony ends with the **Anand Sahib** (Hymn of Bliss) and **karah parshad** is given to the congregation.

Initiation into the Khalsa

Boys and girls aged fourteen or sixteen are able to join the **Khalsa**. These Sikhs must have the **panj kakke** – the five Ks.

The ceremony is called **Amrit** and is conducted by five members of the Sikh community, representing the **panj piare**. They wear robes: tunics in orange or saffron, a blue sash around their waist and over the shoulder and a blue or orange turban.

One of the five Khalsa members explains the principles of the Sikh faith and reminds the candidates of the teachings of the Guru Granth Sahib Ji. The candidates for initiation are asked if they accept these. The five members of the Khalsa then kneel around an iron bowl, and prepare amrit from sugar and water. The liquid is stirred with a **khanda** (a double-edged sword).

Learning about religion

❶ What ceremonies take place when a Sikh baby is born and why?

❷ a What do people have to do to join the Khalsa?

b Describe the Amrit ceremony.

❸ Why might joining the Khalsa be so important for a Sikh?

Learning from religion

❶ Do you think that it is a good idea for all young children to be brought up within a religion? Explain your views.

❷ Why do you think many teenagers make a special promise to be a member of a religion?

❸ Do you think it would be a good idea if all people had to make this sort of promise when they are teenagers?

Marriage

In this section you will:

● learn about the Sikh marriage ceremony

● consider how marriage ceremonies affect people and why they are important.

Marriage is a very important part of **Sikhism**. Sometimes two families may bring a couple together, but the couple both have the right not to marry. Sikhs believe it is important that the families can get on with each other. This is why Sikhs do not encourage people to marry outside of their religion.

There is sometimes an engagement ceremony in the **gurdwara**, where God is thanked for bringing the couple together. After this, the groom's mother visits the bride and gives her a gold ring to wear.

Anand karaj – the wedding ceremony

A Sikh wedding usually takes place in the morning. It is held in front of a copy of the **Guru Granth Sahib Ji**. In India a bride may be dressed in red, but elsewhere the bride may wear white and be dressed very simply. Her head will be covered with a chunni (scarf). The groom wears a coloured **turban** and scarf and carries a **kirpan**.

A Sikh wedding in India

The Lavan ceremony in Britain

Before the service begins there is a ceremony called the **Milna**. The two families meet and give gifts and then eat a meal.

The ceremony begins with the morning hymn **Asa di var** and **Ardas**.

The first part explains that marriage is not just a social contract but the joining together of two souls.

The bride and groom bow to the Guru Granth Sahib Ji to show that they accept these teachings and want to spend the rest of their lives together.

The bride's father places flower garlands over the couple and then takes one end of the groom's scarf and ties it to the end of the bride's head scarf. This shows that she is leaving her father and joining her husband.

The **Lavan** (wedding hymn) of Guru Ram Das Ji is sung and after each of the four verses the couple walk clockwise around the Guru Granth Sahib Ji, the bride following the groom. Each time, they bow to the Guru Granth Sahib Ji.

The service ends with the sharing of **karah parshad**.

Everyone eats a meal in the **langar** after the ceremony.

Sikhs are expected to remain faithful to their husband or wife, and marriage is important to Sikhs because of strengthening family life and bringing up children. Sikhs accept that divorce is sometimes inevitable. Widows and widowers are allowed to remarry in a gurdwara.

Learning about religion

❶ a What is an 'arranged marriage'?

   b Why might Sikhs not want their children to marry non-Sikhs?

❷ Describe what happens during the Anand karaj.

❸ Why do you think marriage is such an important aspect of Sikhism?

Learning from religion

❶ a Why might some people think arranged marriages are a good idea while others do not?

   b Why might some people prefer to have a religious wedding ceremony rather than marry in a register office (a civil ceremony)?

❷ Write down the vows and promises that you think people should make to each other when they get married.

Death

In this section you will:

● learn the Sikh teachings about death

● consider how Sikh funeral ceremonies affect people and why they are important.

For Sikhs, death is not the end. They believe in eternal life, or **reincarnation**. This means that a soul may be reborn many times as a human or an animal.

The **Guru Granth Sahib Ji** teaches that the body is clothing for the soul and so is not important, just as we might throw away old clothes.

Usually, Sikhs cremate their dead. In India this often happens on the day when someone dies, but elsewhere it may take place two or three days later, so that people have the chance to travel to the funeral.

When someone is dying their friends and relatives will come to their bedside and say **Sukhmani** (the Hymn of Peace).

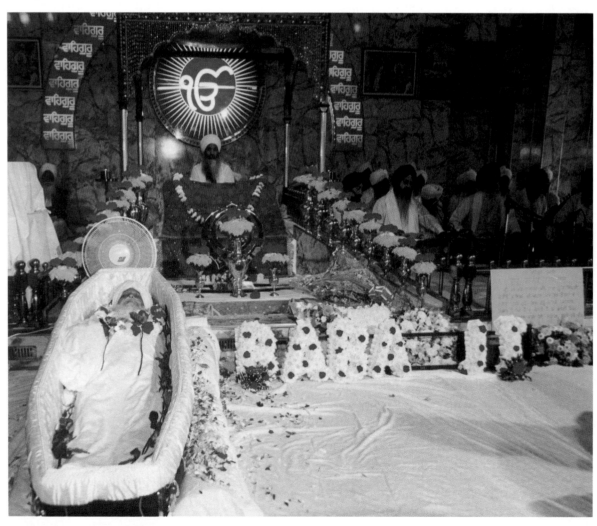

A Sikh funeral ceremony – the body is placed in front of the Guru Granth Sahib Ji

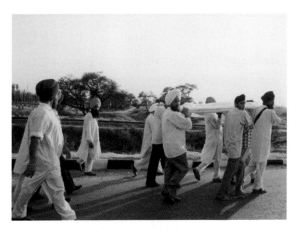

The body is taken for cremation

The dying person will try to reply **Waheguru** (Wonderful Lord). The dead body is washed and dressed in traditional Sikh clothing, including the **five Ks – panj kakke**. It is placed in a coffin and taken to the **gurdwara**.

The coffin is carried to the cremation ground while hymns are sung. In India it is placed on a funeral pyre which is then lit by a close relative. As the coffin burns, someone says the evening prayer – the **Kirtan Sohila**:

All must receive their last call from the Master; daily he summons those souls who must go.

Hold in remembrance the Lord who will summon you; soon you will hear his command.

Kirtan Sohila

This shows the belief that death is just a short sleep before rebirth and that everyone must remember God in the hope of reaching **mukti**.

The relatives and friends of the dead person now return to the gurdwara where the **Anand Sahib** is sung, and **Ardas** is said. The ceremony ends with **karah parshad**.

Mourning

During the next ten days many families stay at home and are visited by friends and relatives. Karah parshad and **langar** are prepared by the family and offered to all visitors.

Some families arrange an **Akhand Path** (complete reading) or **Sadharan Path** (non-continuous reading) of the Guru Granth Sahib Ji after a funeral.

Learning about religion

❶ a What is meant by rebirth and mukti?

   b Why are these ideas so important for Sikhs?

❷ Why do you think Sikhs spend ten days in mourning after the cremation?

Learning from religion

❶ a Why do you think that some people are cremated while others are buried?

   b Do you think the Sikh teaching that the body is unimportant could be helpful to other people? Explain why.

❷ How might a religious ceremony help people when someone dies?

❸ Do you think a period of mourning is a good idea or should people try to get back to normal lives as soon as possible?

Creation

In this section you will:

● learn what Sikhs believe about the creation

● consider the importance of these beliefs and how they affect people's attitudes.

Sikhism is based on the 'Oneness of Creation'. Sikhs believe that the universe was made by God who created the earth and all forms of life on it. God is in charge and arranges the birth, life and death of everything.

Humans, trees, holy places
Coasts, clouds, fields
Islands, continents, universes
Spheres and solar systems

Life forms – egg-born, womb-born, earth-born, sweat-born Only God knows their existence in oceans, mountains, everywhere Nanak says God created them
and God takes care of them all.

Guru Granth Sahib Ji

Before the creation there was no earth, no sky, no sun and no life. Only God existed alone until God's decision to create the world. Then God created everything by a single word:

God spoke once and there was creation.

God is responsible for all of creation and everything in and on the earth belongs to God. God is in charge of all life and without God's **Hukam** (will) nothing can exist, change or develop.

God still looks after the world and protects it and Sikhism believes that all creatures lead their lives under God's rule.

If I were a doe living in the forest, eating grass and leaves, with God's Grace I will find God.
If I were a cuckoo living in the mango tree, contemplating and singing, God reveals through God's mercy.
If I were a female snake, dwelling in the ground, let God's word be in my being, my dread would vanish.
Eternal God is found, light meets light.

Guru Granth Sahib Ji

Sikhism teaches that God created five elements – air, water, earth, fire and space. Everything in nature is made from these elements. Water is the most important of the elements, but they must all be kept in balance to avoid disaster.

Learning about religion

❶ What do Sikhs believe about creation?

❷ a What does Sikhism teach about the relationship between God and animals?

   b How does God take care of the world according to Sikh teaching?

❸ Why are these beliefs about creation important for Sikhs?

Learning from religion

❶ All religions have stories about how the world was created. Why do you think this is?

❷ Does it matter if these stories are true or not? Why?

❸ Explain how you believe the world was created.

Environment

In this section you will:

● learn how Sikhs care for the environment

● learn why this is important for Sikhs and what we might learn from these teachings.

Sikhs believe that God created the world as a place where every type of plant and animal could live so that all life could have the chance to prove that it was good enough to reach **mukti**.

Guru Nanak Dev Ji taught that:

Nature we see
Nature we hear
Nature we observe with awe, wonder and joy

Nature in the nether regions
Nature in the skies
Nature in the whole creation
Nature in the sacred texts (Vedas, Puranas and Qur'an)
Nature in all reflection
Nature in food, in water, in garments and in love for all
Nature in species, kinds, colours
Nature in life forms
Nature in good deeds
Nature in pride and in ego
Nature in air, water and fire
Nature in the soil of the earth
All nature is yours, O powerful Creator
You command it, observe it and pervade within it.

Guru Granth Sahib Ji

Sikhs believe that humans are the stewards of the earth and have to look

Sikhs working to save the environment

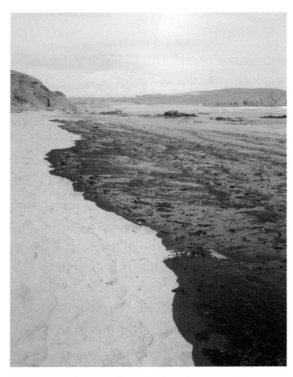

Sikhs condemn oil pollution because it damages the environment

after it. They also believe that God's spirit is in everything, and therefore many Sikhs are vegetarians.

Sikhs believe that they must take care not to disturb the balance of nature. In the Punjab, rainfall is vital and always welcomed. When the monsoon arrives Sikhs celebrate because God has been good to them.

Sikhs are forbidden to kill for the sake of killing.

The Gurus have strongly made us aware of our responsibility towards this earth.

Guru Granth Sahib Ji

Sikhs believe that the environment can only be preserved if the balance God created is maintained. The principles for this are found in the Guru Granth Sahib Ji:

Pray to God – remember God and God's authority always;

Earn an honest living – do not take what does not belong to you, or more than you need – essential truths for a proper relationship with nature;

Share with others – this includes all creation, not just human beings.

Guru Granth Sahib Ji

Learning about religion

❶ a What is the environment?

b What is a steward?

❷ a Why do Sikhs give thanks when the monsoon arrives?

b Why are Sikhs forbidden to kill for fun or sport?

❸ Why do you think the Sikh teaching about caring for the environment is important?

Learning from religion

❶ Why do you think people are so concerned about the environment? Do you think people should be more concerned?

❷ How might non-Sikhs carry out some of these ideas about caring for the environment?

❸ 'Other animals are just as important as human beings.' Do you agree or disagree?

Human rights

In this section you will:

● consider the importance of Sikh teachings about human rights

● learn what Sikhism says about equality, and how this affects people.

It is a very important teaching of **Sikhism** that everyone is equal regardless of race, sex, class, **caste** or religion. Any hungry person who visits a **gurdwara** will always be fed.

Sikhs believe that God, who is the creator and source of all forms of life, is without any form, gender or colour. Any differences between humans are unimportant – they do not make any one person better than any other. Any act of kindness which is performed towards another human being is seen as an act of worship to God.

Guru Nanak Dev Ji was born a Hindu, and Sikhism has kept some of the teachings of Hinduism. For example, Hinduism also welcomes people of all religious beliefs. However, Guru Nanak Dev Ji taught that the caste system of Hinduism was wrong.

There are four varnas (castes) which form divisions within Hindu society. Within these varnas, there are also many jati (caste groups). Hindus believe that every Hindu is born into a particular caste because of their behaviour in a previous life and that these cannot be changed.

The caste system affects almost everything a Hindu does. Marriages should only take place between members of the same caste. Some Hindus will not eat with, or take food from, members of castes lower than theirs.

Guru Nanak Dev Ji wanted the caste system to be abolished. Unfortunately some people still believe that it is important and it can sometimes influence aspects of Sikh life such as marriage, where members of one group may be unwilling to marry a member of another.

However, Sikhs are taught to treat all people equally and hope to be treated the same.

A Hindu Brahmin during Divali. Guru Nanak Dev Ji taught that the caste system was wrong

The langar is a place where Sikhs can offer hospitality to all

A Sikh independent homeland

One of the major problems for Sikhs today in seeking equality is Khalistan. In 1799 CE Maharaja Ranjit Singh established Lahore as the capital of an independent Sikh state where true equality among Sikhs, Muslims, Hindus and others was practised. The British took over the Punjab in 1849 CE and ended Sikh independence. When India became independent from Britain in 1947 CE, two countries were established: India was mainly Hindu and Pakistan was mainly Muslim. The Punjab was split between India and Pakistan. Sikhs asked for independence but it was not given to them. In 1966 CE the Indian government agreed that the province of the Punjab should have Punjabi as its official language and that Sikhs should represent the province in the Punjabi Suba (assembly). However, Sikhs are still working to reunite the Punjab into one country of their own.

Learning about religion

❶ What do Sikhs teach about equality?

❷ a What is the Hindu caste system?

   b Why do Sikhs believe that the caste system is wrong? How does the langar show this belief in action?

Learning from religion

❶ a Why do you think that some people are not treated equally?

   b Do you think that everyone should follow the Sikh teaching about equality?

❷ Explain what you might do to try to make sure that everyone is treated equally.

Service to others 1 – sewa

In this section you will:

● learn why the idea of sewa is so important to Sikhs

● consider how this teaching might affect people.

It is very important for all Sikhs to provide a service to the community – **sewa**. This includes service to the Sikh community itself and others. Sikhs should give up some of their time and energy to help others. **Sikhism** comprises service to God, to the **Khalsa** and to all of humanity.

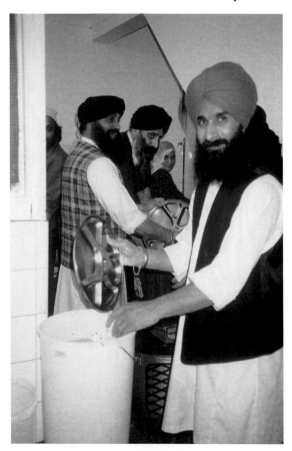

Tan – physical service: helping in the langar

Sikhism teaches that a person should try to become less self-centred (**manmukh**) and more God-centred (**gurmukh**) and so live their lives to help others (sewa).

Although **Nam Simran** (remembering God) is central to Sikhism, this must be combined with sewa. The following words from the **Guru Granth Sahib Ji** emphasize this point:

> True worship consists in the meditation of God's name … There can be no worship without performing good deeds.
>
> Guru Granth Sahib Ji

There are three different aspects of sewa:

● **Tan** – this is physical service and might include working in the **langar** and helping to look after the **gurdwara**. Providing langar for the congregation is seen as a privilege as well as a duty.

● **Man** – this is mental service. Sikhs might do this by studying the Guru Granth Sahib Ji and teaching it to others.

● **Dhan** – this is material service to other people. Sikhs might give money to charities or give their time to help people who are in need. It might also include building a school or a hospital, visiting the sick or caring for disaster victims.

All of these services should be performed because a Sikh wants to serve God. Therefore, Sikhs can perform sewa and so serve God and the world.

Tan – physical service: sweeping the pavements of the Golden Temple

The Gurus set the example of sewa by performing basic tasks which some people would have considered to be beneath them, for example cleaning the gurdwara.

A place in God's court can only be attained if we do service to others in this world … Wandering ascetics, warriors, celibates, holy men, none of them can obtain **mukti** without performing sewa.

Guru Granth Sahib Ji

Learning about religion

❶ a What is meant by 'sewa'?

 b Why is this such an important part of Sikhism?

❷ What types of sewa might a Sikh be involved in to help the community?

❸ Which do you think is the most important of the three types of sewa? Write down your thoughts.

Learning from religion

❶ a Do you think that working to help other people is important? Give your reasons.

 b Do you think that it might help if everyone followed the Sikh teaching about sewa?

❷ How might practising sewa help you feel closer to God?

Service to others 2

In this section you will:

● learn about Sikh principles of life

● consider how these principles affect Sikhs and why they are important.

The **Gurus** said that Sikhs should live their lives according to three principles which are all equally important:

● **Nam Simran** – to remember the name of God. This can be done by meditating on God's name.

● **Kirat karna** – to earn a living by honest means.

● **Vand chhakna** – to share everything in charity with people who are less fortunate.

Sikhs must not think of the religious side of their life as being separate. Prayer, hard work and generosity are all equally important. Sikhs are discouraged from spending all their time on the religious aspects of life, such as prayer. They must live lives which are complete and contribute to the welfare of the community.

Kirat karna

Kirat karna means that Sikhs must earn their living honestly. Everyone has a responsibility to earn a living if they possibly can. It does not matter what the work is, provided that it is honest and not against the teachings of the Gurus. Therefore, a Sikh should never earn money from selling illegal drugs or doing something which might take advantage of other people.

Sikhism teaches that it is not wrong to be rich provided that the money is gained honestly, but that it is wrong to live your life just in order to make a lot of money. The money which a Sikh earns is used for his or her family and also for the **Khalsa** and the community as a whole.

A Sikh hospital in Nairobi

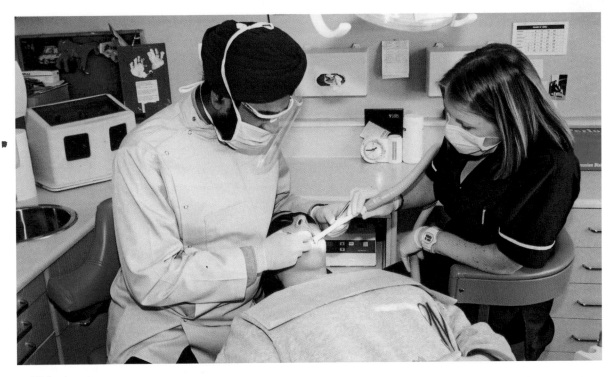

A Sikh dentist

Vand chhakna

Vand chhakna teaches Sikhs that they should live their lives on the principles of generosity and self-sacrifice.

Guru Amar Das Ji taught Sikhs the idea of **daswandh**. This means giving a tenth of spare money to the community. Money given in this way may be used for building schools or hospitals or to help those who are poor or suffering.

Learning about religion

❶ a What is meant by Nam Simran?

  b Why is this an important part of Sikhism?

❷ a What are Kirat karna and Vand chhakna?

  b Why are these as important as Nam Simran?

Learning from religion

❶ a Is it as important to help other people as it is to pray? Why?

  b Do you think that everyone would benefit from the idea of daswandh?

❷ How might you live in order to follow Kirat karna?

❸ How would you try to ensure that you lived a good life?

Women in Sikhism

In this section you will:

● learn about the Sikh attitude towards women

● learn why this is such an important part of Sikh life and teaching.

Sikhism is one of the few religions where women have an equal role with men.

A Sikh woman can choose her own way of life, and many continue their education to university in order to fulfil their ambition for a professional career.

Where there is any suggestion that Sikhism is treating women differently from men, this is because of society and history and goes against the teachings of the **Gurus**.

Women can be members of the **Khalsa**, in exactly the same ceremony as men, and can become a **granthi**. The role of women in services in the **gurdwara** is increasing.

The reason why many women did not assist with Sikh ceremonies in the past was due to the general prejudices of the period rather than to any sexist belief.

We are God's own people, neither high nor low nor in between … Religion consists not in mere talk. He who looks on all alike and consider all to be equal is acclaimed as truly religious.

Guru Granth Sahib Ji

Guru Nanak Dev Ji taught that:

From women born, shaped in the womb, to woman betrothed and wed;
We are bound to women by ties of affection, on women man's future depends.
If one woman dies he seeks another; with a woman he orders his life.
Why then should one speak evil of women, they who give birth to kings?

Guru Granth Sahib Ji

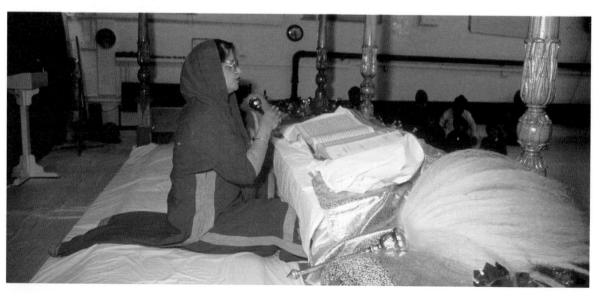

A women granthi leading the worship in the gurdwara

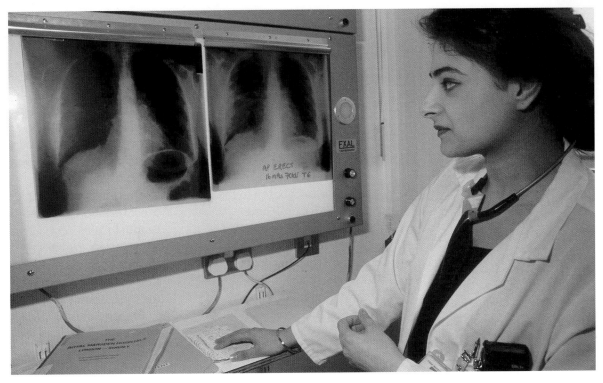

A Sikh doctor

The Gurus also taught that people should not follow the Hindu practice of giving dowries to a man in order to marry a particular woman. They also condemned suttee – the idea that when a man dies his wife should kill herself on his funeral pyre.

Learning about religion

❶ **a** What is meant by sexism?

   b How is the Sikh attitude towards women different from that in some other religions?

❷ What did Guru Nanak Dev Ji teach about women?

❸ Why is the Sikh teaching about the role of women important?

Learning from religion

❶ **a** Why do you think that some people treat women differently from men?

   b Do you think that the Sikh teaching about the role of women should be adopted by other people?

❷ 'Although women and men are equal, they have different roles to play and so may not be treated the same.' Do you agree?

Glossary

Adi Granth a collection of the hymns of the first four Gurus and some of those of Guru Arjan Dev Ji

A hankar pride

Akal Takht 'Throne of the Eternal'. The building facing the Golden Temple in Amritsar

Akhand Path a continuous reading of the Guru Granth Sahib Ji from beginning to end

Amrit 'nectar'. Sanctified liquid made of sugar and water, used in initiation ceremonies

Amritsar a city in the Punjab and the location of the Golden Temple

Amritvela early morning prayer and meditation

Anand Sahib 'Hymn of bliss'

Anandpur Sahib a town in a valley at the foot of the Himalayas. The ashes of the head of Guru Tegh Bahadur Ji are buried there. It is also the place where Guru Gobind Singh Ji founded the Khalsa

Ardas the prayer offered during most religious acts

Asa di var the morning hymn

Baisakhi a major Sikh festival celebrating the foundation of the Khalsa in 1699

Belief accepting that something is true

Bhakti devotion to God, worship

Caste the Hindu belief that people are born into different social groups

Chanani a canopy over the scriptures, used as a mark of respect

Chauri a symbol of the authority of the Guru Granth Sahib Ji. A fin waved over scriptures, made of yak hair or nylon

Dasam Granth a collection of compositions, some of which are attributed to the tenth Sikh Guru, Guru Gobind Singh Ji, compiled some years after his death

Daswandh giving a tenth of surplus money to the community

Dhan material service to other people

Divali Mela the festival which marks the end of the rainy season and the escape and return to Amritsar of Guru Har Gobind Ji

Diwan congregational worship

Faith believing or trusting in something

Five Ks *see* Panj kakke

Goindwal the location of a deep well, or baoli, built by Guru Amar Das Ji

Golak a long box in which worshippers place their offerings of money

Granthi a reader of the Guru Granth Sahib Ji, who officiates at ceremonies

Gurbani the word of God revealed by the Gurus. Also the Shabads, contained in the Guru Granth Sahib Ji

Gurdwara Sikh place of worship. Literally the 'doorway to the Guru'

Gurmukh someone who lives by the Gurus' teaching

Gurmukhi 'from the Guru's mouth'. The name given to the script in which the scriptures and the Punjabi language are written

Gurpurb a Guru's anniversary (birth or death). This term is also used for other anniversaries, for example the installation of the Adi Granth in 1604 CE

Guru a teacher. In Sikhism, the title of Guru is used for the ten human Gurus and the Guru Granth Sahib Ji

Guru Granth Sahib Ji the Sikh scriptures, compiled by Guru Arjan Dev Ji and given its final form by Guru Gobind Singh Ji

Guru Nanak Dev Ji (1469–1539 CE) the first Guru and the founder of the Sikh faith

Gutka a collection of Sikh hymns

Harimandir Sahib the Golden Temple in Amritsar

Hola Mohalla Mela the festival which celebrates Guru Gobind Singh Ji holding a three-day festival at Anandpur

Hukam 'God's will'

Ik Onkar 'There is only One God'. The first phrase of the Mool Mantar. It is also used as a symbol to decorate Sikh objects

Japji Sahib a morning prayer, composed by Guru Nanak Dev Ji, which forms the first chapter of the Guru Granth Sahib Ji

Kachera traditional underwear/shorts. One of the five Ks

Kam lust or desire

Kangha a comb worn in the hair. One of the five Ks

Kara a steel band, worn on the right wrist. One of the five Ks

Karah parshad sanctified food distributed at Sikh ceremonies

Karma actions and their consequences

Karodh anger

Kaur 'Princess'. Name given to all Sikh females

Kesh uncut hair. One of the five Ks

Khalsa 'The community of the pure'. The Sikh community

Khanda a double-edged sword used in the initiation ceremony. Also used as the emblem on the Sikh flag

Kirat karna earning one's livelihood by one's own efforts

Kirpan a sword. One of the five Ks

Kirtan devotional singing of the compositions found in the Guru Granth Sahib Ji

Kirtan Sohila a prayer said before going to sleep. It is also used at the cremation ceremony and when the Guru Granth Sahib Ji is laid to rest

Langar 'Guru's kitchen'. The gurdwara dining hall and the food served in it

Lavan four verses which are sung at a wedding ceremony

Lobh greed

Mala prayer beads

Man mental service

Manji the small platform on which the scripture is placed

Manmukh thinking about oneself first

Maya delusion, looking at the world and ignoring God

Mela 'fair'. Used of Sikh festivals which are not gurpurbs

Milna the ceremony which takes place before the wedding service

Moh being too attached to the world

Mool Mantar 'basic teaching'. The basic statement of belief at the beginning of the Guru Granth Sahib Ji

Mukti escape from rebirth

Nam Japna remembering the name of God

Nam Simran meditation on the divine name, using passages of scripture

Nishan Sahib the Sikh flag, flown at gurdwaras

Nit nem saying the specified daily prayers

Pakha a fan used by Sikhs walking with the Gurus, keeping them cool in the hot areas of the Punjab

Palanquin a special carriage

Panj kakke 'the five Ks'. The symbols of Sikhism worn by Sikhs

Panj piare 'the five beloved ones'. Those first initiated into the Khalsa and those who perform the rite today

Ragi a Sikh musician who sings compositions from the Guru Granth Sahib Ji

Reincarnation the belief that people are reborn after their death

Romalla a cloth on which the Guru Granth Sahib Ji is placed

Sadharan Path non-continuous reading of the Guru Granth Sahib Ji after a funeral

Sadhsangat congregation or assembly of Sikhs

Sahaj-dhari 'seekers after God'. Sikhs who are not members of the Khalsa

Sahib term of respect

Serovar the pool around the Golden Temple in Amritsar

Sewa service directed at the sadhsangat and gurdwara, but also to humanity in general

Shabad a hymn from the Guru Granth Sahib Ji, the divine word

Sikhism the religion of the Sikhs

Singh 'Lion'. Name adopted by Sikh males

Sodar Rahiras the prayer said before the evening meal

Sukhmani the Hymn of Peace

Tan physical service

Trust having confidence in something

Turban head covering worn by many Sikhs

Vand chhakna sharing one's time, talents and earnings with the less fortunate

Waheguru 'Wonderful Lord'. A Sikh name for God

Yatras visits to places associated with the Gurus and Sikhism

Index